SHE WENT TO SPACE

Maine Astronaut JESSICA MEIR

FRAN HODGKINS

Down East Books
Camden, Maine

DownEastBooks

An imprint of The Globe Pequot Publishing Group, Inc.
64 South Main Street
Essex, CT 06426
www.globepequot.com

Distributed by NATIONAL BOOK NETWORK

Copyright © 2024 by Fran Hodgkins
Interior design by Lynda Chilton, Chilton Creative

British Library Cataloguing in Publication Information available

Library of Congress Cataloging-in-Publication Data Available

ISBN 9781684750726 (cloth : alk. paper) | ISBN 9781684750733 (epub)

Printed in India

The sky was black. It wasn't the sky, really. It was space. And Jessica Meir was stepping out into it. Cold, dark, empty. More than 200 miles below, Earth shone blue and green and white.

This was where a lifetime of dreams had led. To being an astronaut.

Jessica's story starts on July 1, 1977, when she was born in Caribou, Maine. Caribou is in Aroostook County, not far from Canada. The night sky there is full of stars.

Her parents were immigrants. Her mother, Ulla-Britt Karlsson, had been a nurse in Sweden. While at work, she met a very interesting man: Josef Meir, a Jewish Iraqi man whose family had fled Baghdad due to anti-Semitism. They went to Beirut, Lebanon, where he studied at the American University. After taking part in the 1948 Arab-Israeli War, Josef went to medical school in Switzerland. Then, he found a job at the Swedish hospital where Ulla-Britt worked.

They married in Sweden and had two daughters. Then Josef was accepted to a program at the prestigious Johns Hopkins School of Medicine in Baltimore, Maryland. The family moved to the United States. A job offer drew them to Caribou, where they had three more children—Jessica was the youngest.

Although their backgrounds were quite different, the Meirs gave their daughter complementary interests. From her mother, Jessica received a love of nature and the outdoors. From her father, a sense of adventure and her Jewish faith. "I had this curiosity about the world around me, the natural world, particularly the plants and the animals," she recalled. "And perhaps that was because I grew up in this remote town, lots of forest around, my mom being Swedish—Swedes often have this innate connection and a close connection to nature. I loved biology."

When Jessica was five, she watched a space shuttle launch on TV. The space shuttles were reusable craft that launched into space by piggybacking on a rocket and returned to Earth like a plane. The launch made Jessica realize that she wanted to be an astronaut.

How do you get the world's toughest job? It's not easy!

IMAGINE THIS GROUP OF PEOPLE WANT TO BE ASTRONAUTS.

NASA requires that you

☐ Be a U.S. citizen

☐ Have a master's degree . . .

☐ . . . in a STEM field.

A master's degree is the next degree you get after finishing college.

STEM fields include engineering, biological science, physical science, computer science or math.

☐ Have at least two years of experience that you got after your degree . . .

☐ . . . or at least 1,000 hours pilot-in-command time on jet aircraft.

OR you can have a finished medical degree, two years of work toward a Ph.D. in STEM, or completion of test pilot school.

And finally:

☐ Pass the NASA physical.

Being smart and healthy isn't enough, though. Astronauts also need to communicate well, work well with others (spacecraft are small on the inside!), and be good leaders.

How does NASA figure this out? Hopefuls must pass a lot of tests. And that's not the end—the people who pass are considered Astronaut Candidates. Then, NASA employees review the applications. Some lucky candidates get invited to NASA for interviews. They get asked questions like:

☐ Why do you want to become an astronaut?
☐ Do you know how to fix things, like a car or a computer?
☐ How do you react to change?
☐ Will you be a good representative of NASA once you are an astronaut?
☐ Do you know how to blend into a group, act as a team?
☐ Who are you as a person?

Since the 1960s, only 350 people have been astronauts. They were all men until Sally Ride became the first American woman in space in 1983 (two other women had been Soviet cosmonauts).

The odds are against anyone becoming an astronaut. But Jessica had a plan!

People called her "Space Girl" at Brown!

Growing up in Caribou gave her time to enjoy the outdoors. She learned to ski early, and later went on to learn how to skydive and SCUBA dive, including diving under ice in Antarctica. "The happiest and most content I've ever been has been when I have the mental and physical challenges at the same time. I've always been this way, and I'm sure my mother would agree." But she doesn't take risks for the thrill of it. "It is more about controlled risk," she says. "I do truly live by the philosophy that without risk, there is no reward."

After she graduated from Caribou High School, Jessica went to Brown University in Rhode Island. and studied biology. Between her freshman and sophomore years, she took part in a special program at NASA, the Space Life Sciences Training Program. For six weeks, she lived in NASA facilities and worked in their space biology labs. She also attended lectures given by astronauts and specialists. "Being exposed to all that I think really helped me realize that this was realistic—I could be involved in space life sciences, or NASA, or maybe even being an astronaut."

She studied hard and took advantage of any opportunities that came her way. She worked in the lab of a researcher who was investigating bio-artificial muscles. She designed an experiment and submitted it to NASA and won a place in a special program. The program involves a plane called the "Vomit Comet," because it makes some people sick as it flies up and down in a series of peaks and dips. At the peak, the pilots cut the engines and the plane falls. The people inside experience about 30 seconds of weightlessness before the engines start again.

She graduated from Brown in 1999 with her bachelor's degree. She then went to the International Space University in France for a master's degree. While she was there, NASA called again— would she like to come to the Johnson Space Center in Houston, to work in the human physiology program?

Why, yes! She spent three years there, running experiments designed by other scientists to find out how conditions in outer space affect the human body.

Space isn't kind to the human body! Without gravity to work against, muscles get weak, and bones lose their strength.

The idea of life in extreme environments fascinated her. So, Jessica went to the Scripps Institution of Oceanography to get her Ph.D. in marine biology.

Wait, wait, you may be thinking. I thought she wanted to be an astronaut. So why is she studying marine biology? As in, sea creatures?

EVEN THOUGH YOU MAY THINK OF SPACE AND THE OCEAN BEING COMPLETE OPPOSITES, THEY'RE MORE ALIKE THAN THEY SEEM AT FIRST GLANCE:

OCEAN	SPACE
Cold	Cold
Dark after the first 300 feet	Dark
You float weightless	You float weightless
Likely to kill you—pressure, no oxygen	Likely to kill you—pressure, no oxygen
Likely to kill you—sharks, venomous fish, etc.	No sharks, no venomous fish
Need special tech to survive	Need special tech to survive
Largely unexplored	Largely unexplored

So, studying the ocean was actually a very smart way to get ready for exploring space.

Jessica focused on some of the world's deep-diving champions: elephant seals and emperor penguins. Diving deep is a very dangerous prospect for any living thing because the water weighs down on every square inch. At the surface, that weight is 1 atmosphere (ATM)—or 14.7 pounds. (We don't feel it because the water inside us is pushing back at the same force.) At 33 feet down, it's two atmospheres. As you keep going, every 33 feet adds an additional atmosphere. Animals that dive deep, like elephant seals and whales, are adapted to these pressures, but people aren't.

At this time, she sent in her first application to be an astronaut.

She made it all the way to the final round, but the answer was no. "You did a great job," said Sunny Williams, the astronaut who called her, "But you're not in the class this time." Jessica was disappointed. "I thought, 'Well, all right, maybe I'll be better off. Maybe this is meant to be. And I'm so lucky I have this other career now. So, I'm going to go on with my life.'"

And that included geese.

Not just any geese: bar-headed geese. These geese make an astonishing migration: they go from their wintering grounds in southern Asia to their nesting grounds in central Asia. What makes that remarkable is that they must fly over the world's tallest mountain range, the Himalayas!

Working with a flock of imprinted bar-headed geese, Meir raised them and trained them to fly in a special wind tunnel that modeled the low-oxygen conditions over the mountains. It was the first time scientists had ever studied the birds' physiology. Jessica and her fellow researchers found that the birds were better suited for high altitudes than typical mammals because of the way their bodies, especially their heart and lungs, work.

When a gosling or duckling hatches, it becomes immediately attached to the first thing it sees. This is called "imprinting."

In 2012, she joined the faculty at Harvard Medical School and Massachusetts General Hospital as an associate professor, continuing her work on comparative physiology. Many people would have decided they'd reached the top of the mountain—a position teaching at one of the world's most prestigious medical schools. Yet Jessica was not done. She was still on Earth.

In 2013, she applied again for the Astronaut Corps. Again, she went through the exhaustive (and exhausting!) process of interviews, physicals, and tests. More than 6,000 people had applied. As she worked in her lab at the hospital, her cell phone rang. It was a Houston number. Would it be a yes, or another no?

It was a yes!

66 *It's difficult to process that the dream that I'd had since I was five years old could have actually come true.* 99

But she couldn't share the news yet—all the applicants had to be notified, and then a public announcement had to be made.

Jessica's astronaut class, the class of 2013, was the first astronaut class that was half women and half men. She was one of eight members in the class.

The training lasted two years. It focused on flight training, Russian language training—everybody on the International Space Station (ISS) must speak English and Russian—and all the different systems on the ISS. She learned how to use the ISS's robotic arm. And she learned how to use a spacesuit by spending time, fully suited up, in a big swimming pool. Astronauts also learn survival and leadership skills.

After waiting since she was five years old, Jessica went to space on September 25, 2019, riding to the ISS in a Soyuz space capsule. Because of her dual citizenship, she became the first Swede in space. She stayed on the ISS for two missions, Expedition 61 and Expedition 62.

Astronauts can bring a few personal items with them to the ISS. Among the items she brought were her piccolo and socks with menorahs on them— which created an online buzz when she posted with them for Hannukah.

Jessica made history. She and fellow astronaut Christina Koch made the first spacewalk made solely by women. For 7 hours and 17 minutes, they worked to replace a power unit that wasn't working. Christina had made other spacewalks, but this was Jessica's first ever—but not her last. She made three more space-walks, spending more than 21 hours outside of the space station.

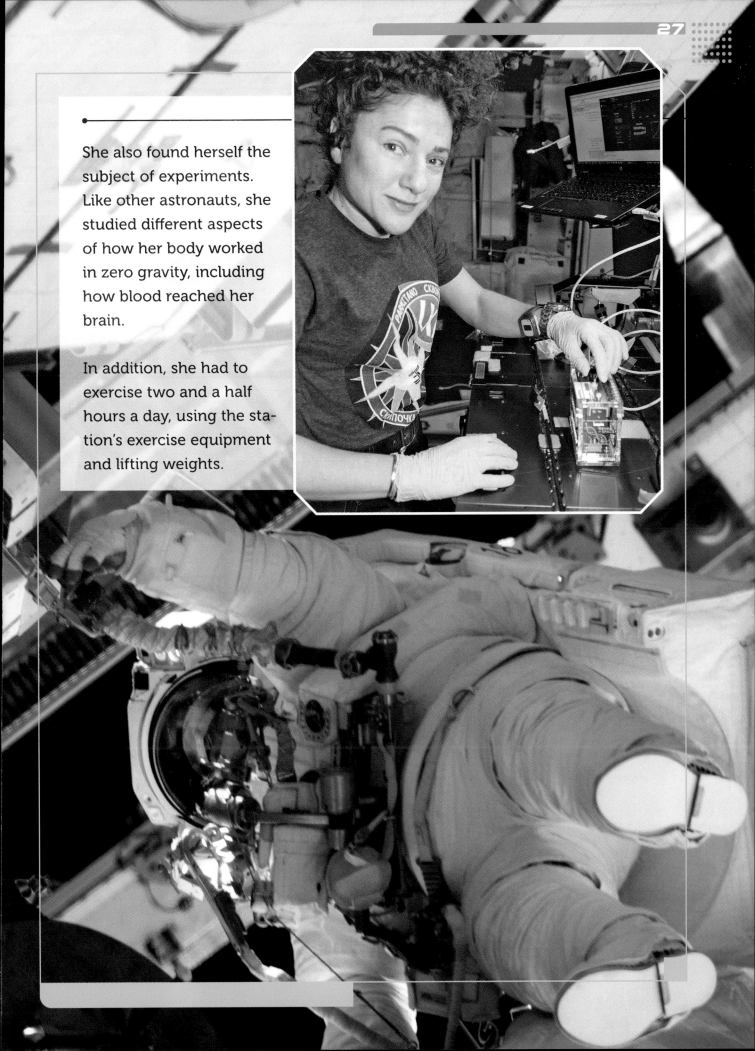

She also found herself the subject of experiments. Like other astronauts, she studied different aspects of how her body worked in zero gravity, including how blood reached her brain.

In addition, she had to exercise two and a half hours a day, using the station's exercise equipment and lifting weights.

Jessica left the ISS on April 17, 2020—after a total of 205 days in space. During that time, the space station made 3,280 orbits around the earth, and within it, Jessica traveled 86.9 million miles. She became one of just a handful of astronauts to have spent so long in space.

Upon their return, Jessica and the other astronauts found life on Earth was hugely different from when they had left. When Jessica had headed for the ISS, no one had even heard of COVID. When they returned, they found quarantines and lock-downs in place. The recovery crew who met their capsule in Kazakhstan wore face masks and latex gloves. After a medical checkup, she and Andrew Morgan, another NASA astronaut, were taken 200 miles to an airport that was open to international flights (their cosmonaut companion, Oleg Skripochka, went to Moscow).

> **We were really the only three humans that were not subject to Covid concerns at the time. Billions of humans were dealing with this in some way or another, and the three of us weren't.**

Within months of her return, Jessica went back to work. When she's not in space, she does much of the same work as other astronauts. She's done a lot: Assistant to the Chief Astronaut for the Human Landing System, which is building the next lunar lander; Deputy for the Flight Integration Division, and Assistant to the Chief Astronaut for Commercial Crew. She's also been the Commander for a Desert Research and Technology mission in 2022.

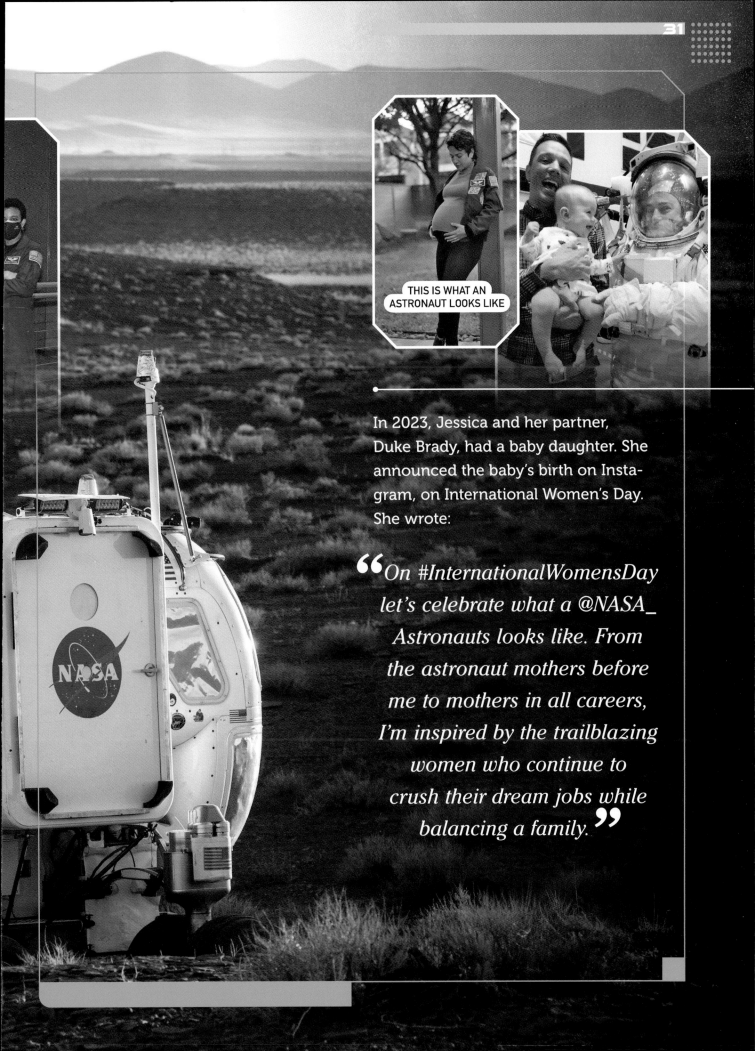

THIS IS WHAT AN
ASTRONAUT LOOKS LIKE

In 2023, Jessica and her partner, Duke Brady, had a baby daughter. She announced the baby's birth on Instagram, on International Women's Day. She wrote:

On #InternationalWomensDay let's celebrate what a @NASA_ Astronauts looks like. From the astronaut mothers before me to mothers in all careers, I'm inspired by the trailblazing women who continue to crush their dream jobs while balancing a family.

What's next for Jessica Meir? Will she go to the Moon? Will she go to Mars? While she wasn't selected for NASA's first trip back to the moon, the possibilities are endless. She wants to keep exploring for all of us—including her daughter.

One thing that Jessica believes is,

"Make sure you are doing what you are most passionate about, not what you think you should be doing or what your parents want you to do. If you're not pursuing something you're passionate about, you're not going to excel at it, and you're not going to be happy.

Also, be aware you need to push yourself, go outside of your comfort zone."

After all, like the astronaut says: No risk, no reward.